THE BATSFORD COLOUR BOOK OF LONDON

THE BATSFORD COLOUR BOOK OF

London

Introduction and commentaries by Garry Hogg

B. T. BATSFORD LTD   LONDON

First published 1971

© B. T. Batsford Ltd 1971

Filmset in Great Britain by Filmtype Services Ltd, Scarborough, Yorkshire
Made and printed in Denmark by F. E. Bording Ltd, Copenhagen
for the publishers B. T. Batsford Ltd, 4 Fitzhardinge Street, London W.1.

7134 0021 8

Contents

Acknowledgments

The Publishers wish to thank the following for permission to reproduce photographs appearing in this book:
British Tourist Authority for page 41
Colour Library International for pages 45, 57 and 71
Fox Photos for page 61
Noel Habgood for pages 47, 67, 91 and 93
A. F. Kersting for pages 37, 39, 69 and 75
Picturepoint for pages 35, 55 and 59
Kenneth Scowen for pages 33, 43, 49, 51, 53, 63, 65, 73, 77, 79, 81, 83, 85, 87, 89 and 95

The map appearing on pages 28-29 was drawn by Arthur Banks.

Introduction

High on his massive column, his back turned to the King Edward VII Gardens, looking down the incomparable Avenida da Liberdade, Sebastião José de Carvalho e Mello, Marquês de Pombal, statesman and architect, contemplates the city which, under his inspiration and guidance, rose phoenix-like from the devastation of the earthquake that overwhelmed Lisbon in 1755 and the inevitable conflagration that immediately followed. He might, with almost more justification than Sir Christopher Wren, who died 60 years before him, have had inscribed on the plinth of his column, '*Si monumentum requiris, circumspice*'. For he was responsible for the renaissance of a city whose ancient heart had been burned out: a small city, it is true; but one of the loveliest, surely, in all Europe? Wren, too, was rebuilding after a devastating fire in a city which is, today, the second largest in the world. But with Wren, the emphasis was on churches: St Paul's represents his major signature, though he designed half a hundred other and lesser churches, many of which survive to this day.

Comparisons, however, are odious. One city can be (as has been said of James Gibbs's charming little church of St Mary-le-Strand) described as 'a casket that one can handle in one's hands'; perhaps Lisbon comes into this category? Another may be so vast that the mind boggles at the effort of coming to terms with it; Tokyo, for instance, the largest city in the world by an ample margin. Rome and Madrid, Brussels and Paris,

8

Oslo and Stockholm, Prague, Bucharest and Amsterdam: all these have their several claims to uniqueness, whether it be that of monumental glory, of preserved medievalism, of the subtle yet dominant interlacing of water and land, the layout of avenues and boulevards, or any other observable and distinctive feature.

Where, in this catalogue, does London stand? It would indeed be a fruitless task to seek to position it accurately in any hierarchy of capital cities. And this fact must surely have been instinctively (or perhaps subconsciously) recognised by those who have spoken and written in praise or criticism of it. Most of those who have committed themselves to considered comment, whether in tribute or otherwise, have, by deliberately avoiding superlatives, left themselves room for manoeuvre.

Abraham Cowley, for instance, a Londoner born, spoke of the city of his birth as 'the Monster'. A disillusioned man, he retired to the country, where soon afterwards he died. Ironically, his body was brought back to London, there to be buried alongside an earlier and greater London-born poet, Edmund Spenser, in Westminster Abbey.

William Cobbett, author of *Rural Rides,* a countryman at heart, indeed the son of a farm labourer and with his roots truly in the soil, somehow contrived to unite the big and the little. For him London was always 'the Great Wen'—a tumour, or cyst, on the gigantic scale, something inevitably monstrous because it was abnormal. Thomas Carlyle, again, writing 200 years after Cowley, called London 'that monstrous tuberosity of civilised life'—and you may make what you will of that unexpected epithet. He wrote as a Scot who moved to London in early middle age; and he must have liked it well enough, for he spent the last half-century of a very long life in Cheyne Walk, Chelsea.

The only writer who has come out fair and square with a categorical superlative, and incidentally the most gracious tribute of all, is William Dunbar. Four and a half centuries ago he wrote:

London, Soveraign of Cities, Semeliest in Sight,
Thou art the Flow'r of Cities all.

And that, surely, is praise indeed; for Dunbar was a Scot, and so you might think he would have placed his own Edinburgh as pre-eminent among cities.

Poets and writers of prose alike, then, have sought to epitomise the emotions aroused in them by this capital city. But always, it would seem, with this reservation of elbow-room, as though they were unwilling to commit themselves to an irrevocable judgment. Spenser, whose 'Sweete Themmes! runne softly till I end my song' is one of the most melodious tributes ever penned to a river, or perhaps to any other natural feature, referred to 'Mery London, my most kyndly nurse'. Alexander Pope took his leave of London with the ambiguous salutation, 'Dear, damned, distracting Town, Farewell!'—though in fact he removed himself no farther from the metropolis than Twickenham. Richard le Gallienne, however, Liverpool-born though not even of English descent, could write 200 years later, with his hand on his heart: 'London, the love of my whole life'.

But it was the great Londoner, Dr Samuel Johnson, who produced the most memorable comment on the city that adopted him and where he is so well remembered and affectionately commemorated. Speaking to his friend Boswell, he uttered the unequivocal judgment: 'When a man is tired of London he is tired of life; for there is in London all that life can afford.'

All that life can afford. True, for here indeed is to be found an *embarras de richesses*. 'Of the making of books (about London) there is no end'; and even if all the books that have ever been written about her were to be assembled between one gigantic pair of covers, nearly as much would perhaps be omitted as included. For London, as Disraeli observed 100 years ago, 'is a nation, not a city'; he also referred to it as 'a modern Babylon', leaving the overtones of the parallel to his listeners' perception. He was himself a Londoner born, and remained a Londoner all his life. Were he alive today, he might well feel it necessary to amplify his comment, for London becomes every day increasingly cosmopolitan.

This leads one to a consideration of how London should be approached. There are cities, capital and otherwise, which should if possible always be approached by water. Among the smaller ones that fall into this category is Valletta. To sail into the open lobster-claw of her Grand Harbour is one of the richer experiences of minor travel. Istanbul is another city which, ideally, is approached by sea, whether down the Bosporus from the Black Sea or by way of the Dardanelles and the Sea of Marmara.

Certainly Lisbon must be included in this tally, for to approach her by way of the wide Tagus estuary until the shadow of the Salazar Bridge falls athwart the deck and the creamy-white buildings of Pombal's city open out in the morning sunlight like some exotic flower is one of the most exquisite of sustained pleasures.

> *Dull would he be of soul who could pass by*
> *A sight so touching in its majesty :*
> *This City now doth, like a garment, wear*
> *The beauty of the morning. . . .*

Wordsworth was writing of London, and of the Thames, as seen from Westminster Bridge—the first bridge to be thrown across the Thames, in 1750, after the succession of London Bridges, and not the one that replaced it some 60 years after he wrote his famous sonnet, the one we know today, that spans the river beneath the shadow of the great tower that houses Big Ben. But the memorable lines spring inevitably to mind as Lisbon slides leisurely into view.

It would not be the same if one were to approach London by way of the river. There are some 40 miles and more of tidal water in this estuary, and as the banks close in on either side they become increasingly infested with the inescapable symbols of industry: the docks and cranes and wharves and warehouses—those controlled by the Port of London Authority extend for some 25 miles along the river—are ever-insistent reminders that this is a great industrial city threaded by its turbid waterway.

Nor would anyone choose to enter London by road or rail if there were a practicable alternative. For the tentacles of her suburbs and outskirts reach out in all directions for endless miles; and these miles are increasing dramatically with every passing year. If he were writing today, old William Cobbett would certainly have to find an epithet for his denigratory 'wen' stronger, more impassioned, than merely 'great'.

No; if possible London should be approached by air, and at night. The experience, however often repeated, is pure magic.

Look how the floor of heaven
Is thick inlaid with patines of bright gold

said Lorenzo to Jessica as they sat together on the moonlit bank. He was speaking of the stars overhead as he sat beside the woman he loved and hoped to marry. But as you fly in to London, from north, south, east or west, you are gliding between these same patines of bright gold and what might be their reflections down below; for the streets and avenues, the squares and crescents and open places are lit with a myriad individual lights that proliferate in whorls and whiplashes and curlicues between the dart-straight lines of the major thoroughfares. As it approaches the runway the plane tilts and rights itself; and the multitudinous stars above you and below tilt and right themselves in sympathy. But now, those that are over your head are no different in size and distribution from what they were and will remain; while the bright gold patines below you become larger, brighter, less detached one from another, and now shed their mantle of faery to become the functional objects they were designed to be. When, next morning, daylight returns and you step out into the great city on which they were shedding their light, they will have withdrawn from the lively scene, their task for the time being fulfilled.

As you looked downwards from your plane you almost certainly caught at least a glimpse of London's river. It has been romantically called 'liquid history', but the metaphor, poetical as it is, does not bear too close scrutiny. Fed by a hundred tributaries upstream, it pours its millions of gallons of water over Teddington Weir, the point at which it ceases to be tidal, and serpentines eastwards through the heart of London beneath bridge after bridge, until it merges with the North Sea, as though heartily glad to have left behind it the restricting shackles of the north and south banks and the bridges alike.

It is true that it has borne on its broad back vessels conveying monarchs and invaders and traitors and innocents to and from the waterside gateways of grim prisons such as The Tower itself. But it could be said that the Thames was only an accessory after the fact; it was on the sidelines while history was being written in stone. So it is perhaps nearer to the truth to state that London herself is a palimpsest of history; not parchment but stonework. For in her very fabric may be seen the irrefutable evidence of 2,000 years of historic existence.

She existed—though admittedly there is no actual tangible evidence of this—long before the Romans came. True, it was nothing more than a small Celtic settlement whose occupants had found for themselves an oasis of firm ground in a marshy area between what later came to be known as Tyburn and Thames. It is a reasonable guess that it had some such name as Llyn-dun, signifying a settlement-near-a-pool, for there are similar names attached to places that are today inhabited by descendants of the Celtic tribes, such as the Welsh.

The first time a recognisable form of the name appears with, so to speak, the cachet of print is in 61 A.D., when the Roman historian Tacitus calls it Londinium. By then, what had been a primitive settlement had been superseded, as was their way, by the Romans under

Emperor Claudius. Tacitus could describe Roman London, somewhat grandiloquently, it would seem, and certainly somewhat prematurely, as 'a famous centre of commerce'. Prematurely, because he had hardly described it thus before Queen Boadicea (her correct name, Boudicca, falls uneasily on the tongue) moved in from East Anglia at the head of her troops and, certainly to the astonishment of the Romans, destroyed the city they had hardly begun to build. They retaliated with characteristic swiftness: the whole tribe of the Iceni were obliterated from the English scene, while Boadicea herself committed suicide in despair.

The Romans learned their lesson. Having completed the erasure of the tribe that had dared to challenge their authority, they set to work to build 'Londinium', adapting the Celtic name to their own style of nomenclature. They had, after all (or so they fondly believed), come to stay; their tradition was always to consolidate their gains, not only by firm rule but by establishing unmistakable visual evidence of their intentions. They proceeded to build for themselves a walled city. The huge rampart they built was some two miles in length and enclosed an area of more than 300 acres. This was the original 'City of London', and it has been authoritatively estimated that even in that remote period in London's history, more than 19 centuries ago, it had a population in excess of 20,000 souls.

Inevitably this lowest stratum that London's buildings present today, the work of the Romans, has been almost entirely overbuilt. You must probe with diligence if you want to see for yourself the handiwork of these great civil engineers who left their mark on so much of western Europe (not forgetting that superb monument to their vision and determination, Hadrian's Wall that spanned northern England between Newcastle upon Tyne and Carlisle).

Certain sites have fortunately been at least partially preserved from the depredations of developers and others. There are portions of this wall round London to be seen incorporated in the Tower, built by William the Conqueror more than five centuries after the Romans' departure from these shores in or about A.D. 410. You will find one of these in the remains of the Wardrobe Tower, just outside the southeast bastion of the great keep, or White Tower as it has long been known.

You will find another, and very fine, portion of the Roman-built wall on the east side of Trinity Square, just to the north of the Tower itself. It is a massive chunk of masonry, in which the characteristic mellow-red tile-like Roman bricks are embedded in what is obviously later, medieval work. But there is no doubt whatsoever that it is Roman work. In fact, Trinity Square is comparatively rich in such relics—an inadequate term, surely, for so massive a sample of Roman building? In the cellar of No. 42 there is a smaller specimen, excellently preserved, which clearly demonstrates this characteristic admixture of brick with quarried ragstone and hewn stone or ashlar.

St Giles Cripplegate, where Oliver Cromwell was married and John Milton buried, offers further evidence of the Romans' building. It is now curiously isolated in the heart of the great Barbican Development Project, just to the north of the long street named London Wall because it lies virtually upon the medieval wall built round the City, and for much of the way on foundations laid many centuries before that wall was planned and built.

At this point there once stood a Roman fortress, established within the perimeter of the earliest wall; on these foundations the church was erected. What remains of both Roman and medieval building on this site is all the more impressive because you can take it in with the eye while looking across it and upwards at some of the ultra-modern blocks of flats and offices that nowadays spring up mushroom-like to write their harsh signature on the impervious sky.

Indeed, it will be found that almost all of the memorable relics of early occupation are to be found in the City—as opposed to the City of Westminster that lies to the west and south, beyond the old city walls. The Romans, opportunist as ever, and with as good an eye for location as any surveyor in any generation since their time, selected two small hills as the twin focal points in the layout of their wall-enclosed city. One of these was Corn Hill, the other was Lud Hill. Near the latter they almost certainly pierced their wall with a gate; we know it today rather as Ludgate (Circus as well as Hill) than simply as Lud Hill; but we retain the name Cornhill to this day.

They selected this site for an excellent reason: it was directly opposite the first point on the tidal Thames which was practicable for crossing by ford. They were not long content, however, to accept the discomfort, and the danger at floodtide and in bad weather, of fording a wide river. They therefore built the first of a succession of timber bridges on that site, just upstream of the Tower of London, and at the point where today Billingsgate Fish Market is located. On the opposite bank, the south bank, there duly came into being a colony—a *sub urbe* of the City proper; we know it today as Southwark. Though bridge succeeded bridge on this important site, and eventually timber was replaced by stone, it remained the only bridge across the Thames for something like 1,600 years.

The Romans abandoned their city, Londinium, in the early years of the fifth century; for hundreds of years thereafter it steadily declined. There were the various Anglo-Saxon invasions, of lesser or greater impact; the Roman tradition was obliterated just as the monumental masonry their craftsmen had produced was largely destroyed to provide the raw material for subsequent building. Cannibalisation of Roman buildings, including, alas, their noblest memorial, Hadrian's Wall, is something that has continued down the centuries in every part of this country in which they originally left their mark. But for the most part it may be assumed that the buildings enclosed by the wall they built to protect this city of theirs on the north bank of the river were of timber. No vestige of these remains today; and this is hardly surprising, for timber buildings are—as was to be seen time and again, and notably in the Great Fire of 1666—inescapably vulnerable to the ravages of fire.

So there is, admittedly, a stratum lacking in this palimpsest of history; there is a long interval during which time dragged by with leaden foot. Scholars tell us that the population of London (the Romans' suffix was soon dropped) dwindled from what it had been during the zenith of their occupation to little more than two-thirds of that figure by the fourteenth century. And this surely is surprising, for by then the Norman Conquest was a thing of the past and England, and London in particular, had once more begun to grow. From the eleventh century onwards, the successive strata become more easily recognisable; they certainly become more memorable.

London has been somewhat oddly termed a congeries of villages. The phrase is not easy to accept in this second half of the twentieth century, even if it may have had some substance in the seventeenth and early eighteenth centuries. Rather, surely, it should be recognised and described as two-cities-in-one. There is the City of London, the famous Square Mile that has evolved within the physical or remembered City Wall; and there is the City of Westminster, the most famous of all the London Boroughs, that occupies the huge area between the City, to the east and Kensington to the west, with its southern boundary running midway between the north and south bank of the Thames.

Between the two of them, with the emphasis inevitably on the latter, it is safe to say that you can see, and without the necessity of painstaking search, examples of the architecture of every historic period from the mid-eleventh century to the present day. Some of the more notable examples of these architectural masterpieces are portrayed in the plates and extended captions that follow. They represent a largely arbitrary choice among the gallimaufry of choices available.

Norman building, so far as London is concerned, is best represented by the magnificent White Tower, in the heart of the Tower of London. But there is also the church of St Bartholomew the Great in Smithfield, founded in 1123 and therefore, with the exception of the chapel in the south-east corner of the White Tower, the oldest church in all London. The Temple Church, too, strictly the church of St Mary the Virgin, dates back to the latter end of the same century, and so may be regarded technically as 'transitional-Norman' in style.

Gothic abounds in generous measure: Westminster Abbey and Westminster Hall, on the north bank, and Southwark Cathedral and Lambeth Palace on the south bank of the river. Of these, the first (though it has been much added to and altered over the years) is generally regarded as London's finest Gothic building after Westminster Abbey. Tudor building, too, is not far behind in quality or in distribution. Perhaps the most impressive example of this is St James's Palace, built by Henry VIII on the site of a building that dates back at least to the year 1100, at which time it existed as a 'hospital for fourteen maidens that are leprous'. The lovely, but much-restored, Staple Inn, in Holborn, is another building of the period; it would be hard to find a stronger contrast between two structures dating from much the same era: the one in mellow brick and stone, the other in sturdy traditional half-timbering.

Evidence of seventeenth-century building is widespread. Among the most notable examples is the famous Banqueting Hall, in Whitehall. The most obvious example, however, and the one that springs most instantly to mind, is Wren's masterpiece, St Paul's Cathedral; it is as essentially the 'City Church' as Westminster Abbey is the church of that other city, to which it gave its name in 1540.

Another notable building of this vital century is Kensington Palace, acquired by William III when he found that St James's Palace was too close to the river for his health. Wren, whose signature is to be found in so many parts of both cities, did a great deal of work on it; what you see of it today, so far as the exterior is concerned at any rate, is largely his handiwork, though William Kent effected elaborate alterations to the interior in the early part of the following century.

Wren was over 90 when he died, so that his activities extended well into the eighteenth century; indeed, it was not until 1710, when he was nearing 80, that he designed and built the splendid brick building we know as Marlborough House, once the home of widowed queens, with its entrance on Pall Mall at its western end. Queen Alexandra lived there after the death of Edward VII, and Queen Mary after the death of George V. Later it was presented by its owners for a permanent Commonwealth Conference Centre. Queen Elizabeth the Queen Mother, therefore, perforce broke the tradition. She now occupies Clarence House (when she is not at her Scottish seat), close to St James's Palace, where her daughter Elizabeth lived with her husband, Prince Philip, before ascending the throne. But this house was built 100 and more years later than Marlborough House, for the occupation of the then Duke of Clarence, who in 1830 was to become William IV.

One of the most splendid buildings to have been built in London in the eighteenth century—in its last quarter—is Somerset House. Today it is largely occupied by government offices, including those of the General Register of 'Hatches, Matches and Dispatches', the Register of Wills and the Audit and Inland Revenue; the gigantic East Wing houses King's College, part of the University of London. You may enter it from the Strand, and certainly the vast and somewhat severe courtyard merits a leisurely inspection; but by far the most imposing view of Somerset House is from the south side of the river, when the enormous and dignified façade rising above the Victoria Embankment comes into its own, immensely impressive. It is interesting to note that before the Royal Academy, the Royal Society and the Society of Antiquaries had their own buildings, all three were housed within the walls of this Palladian edifice, designed and built by Sir William Chambers. Its name derives from the fact that it stands on the site of a palace which the Lord Protector Somerset planned to build for himself 150 years earlier; unfortunately for him, he was executed before he could occupy it.

It is not surprising that with the succeeding centuries more and more buildings of distinction, both large and small, should have proliferated. At one end of the scale, and fairly late in the eighteenth century, there is Somerset House; at the other, and half a century earlier, there is the church of St Martin-in-the-Fields, overlooking Trafalgar Square, one of London's best-loved churches, diminutive in comparison with the great houses and palaces of the era, but with a character and an individuality all its own.

Purists may argue as to the failure of the architect, James Gibbs, to relate the steeple to the main fabric of the church; but that has not prevented St Martin-in-the-Fields from establishing a tradition for fashionable baptisms, weddings and other ceremonies. Charles II was christened here. And here too, in a graveyard virtually obliterated, were buried such disparate individuals as John Hampden (who was also christened here), Nell Gwynn, and the notorious highwayman, Jack Sheppard. Historically-minded visitors will realise that some of those buried here died before James Gibbs's church was built. This emphasises the point already made, here and elsewhere, that churches were often built on sites sanctified by earlier churches. This is one example: an early-eighteenth-century church built on a site that had borne a church since the twelfth century at least. It is an interesting fact that the first religious service ever broadcast, as long ago as 1924, came from St Martin-in-the-Fields.

An even more notable example of this practice is that of St Paul's, built on a site that had borne a church founded in the seventh century by Bishop Mellitus and endowed by King Ethelbert of Kent. It was destroyed by fire in the eleventh century, rebuilt in the same century by the Normans, again destroyed and again rebuilt by the Normans, to survive precariously until fire once again destroyed it in 1666, thus giving Wren his supreme opportunity.

When we come to the nineteenth century, probably the outstanding architectural achievement—though it has always had its critics—is Sir Charles Barry's monumental building in somewhat florid late-Gothic style, the Houses of Parliament, strictly the New Palace of Westminster. The former Houses of Parliament had been almost completely destroyed by fire in 1834, the beautiful Westminster Hall and the crypt of St Stephen's Chapel being virtually the sole survivors. Rebuilding, to Barry's design, began within a very few years; by 1847 the Lords were rehoused, and within the next five years or so Her Majesty's Loyal Commons too had a roof over their head.

As with Somerset House, the finest view of the New Palace of Westminster is unquestionably from the other side of the river, from near or on Lambeth Bridge. From that viewpoint its south façade may be taken in by the eye, and the two great towers, the Victoria and the one always, though erroneously, referred to as 'Big Ben', are to be seen in their best relationship. Incidentally, the somewhat over-ornate tower that rises midway between the two major towers fulfils a minor function as a ventilation-shaft. Those who cynically comment that too much hot air anyway is generated when Parliament is in session may wryly comment to themselves that Sir Charles foresaw this eventuality and made due provision for it.

Another building, hardly less famous, though in a very different context, that dates from the middle of this prolific nineteenth century is the British Museum. It is true that it stands on the foundations of an earlier building, Puget's Montagu House, built in the seventeenth century; but it took the whole of that structure within its ample grasp, then extended it in all directions and eventually demolished the proto-type, in 1852, to present itself with its classical colonnaded façade in that same year. If you wish to restore the balance after too close scrutiny of neo-Gothic in the Houses of Parliament, then you will find the antidote here in Bloomsbury. And if the severe classicism of this impressive façade chills you, once again you can restore the balance by taking a look at the Law Courts, at the junction of Fleet Street and the Strand. For here is an imposing pseudo-Gothic pile, less vast than the Houses of Parliament and smacking faintly also of 'Scottish Baronial': it has an official title, Royal Courts of Justice, and was designed for the Supreme Court of Judicature which had been established in 1873. The designer, G. E. Street, did not live to see its completion, and no one now will ever know whether the *fait accompli* truly matched up to the vision he held in his mind's eye.

Right at the end of this highly productive century an edifice was built that contrasts with virtually every other in London: Westminster Cathedral. Though its date is literally the turn of the century, for it was begun in 1895 and not completed until 1903, the year after the death of its architect, J. F. Bentley, it deliberately echoes what could be termed the 'Early Christian-Byzantine' tradition in building.

It is naturally regarded as the most important (if not necessarily the most beautiful) Roman Catholic structure in the country, though, striking as its exterior is, with its bands of red brick alternating with stripes of white, it will not appeal to all lovers of architectural styles. But no one, however disapproving of the texture of the cathedral as a whole, could fail to admire—in its original sense of wondering-at— the magnificent campanile that lifts out of the close-crowding edifices all about its foot as though minded to take off, spacecraft-wise, for the ultimate confines of the heaven its devout adherents so firmly believe in.

With the turn of the century it would seem that a largely new approach to building became the common denominator of architects and designers. Gone were the Classic (or Gothic, or Byzantine, or what-have-you) influences; now men began anew to think for themselves, to eschew traditions that had sustained architects and given them inspiration over a span of nearly ten centuries. It is true that some of the twentieth-century buildings were to some extent echoes of those that had gone before: County Hall, for instance; and Bush House; and the enormous, multi-windowed Shell-Mex House on the north bank of the Thames, with its gigantic clock, completed between the first and the second world wars.

But already the impulse was towards a 'vertical city'. New discoveries in the manufacture, adaptation and processing of building materials, pre-stressed concrete, toughened glass, strengthened metal alloys, combined with revolutionary building methods and techniques, enabled architects to aim higher, reaching for the skies. The traditionalist finds it hard, if not impossible, to adjust himself to this new concept; he deliberately ignores the protest that building-land is at a premium, that even mere square-footage can often be acquired only at prohibitive prices. Upward building (as on Manhattan Island), therefore, is the only viable answer to the everlasting demand for more and more accommodation, whether for offices or for men and women to live and eat and relax and make love and die with a roof over their heads (however lofty) and four walls to enclose them—however flimsy in appearance compared with the massive stonework of the centuries that have gone before.

These new buildings—and the Millbank Tower, familiarly known as the Vickers Building, is certainly the most elegantly beautiful of them all at the time of writing, though who can say whether it will not have been surpassed both in height and in elegance by the time these words are in print?—have a character of their own. And a dignity. And a splendour.

They are, of course, drastically altering London's skyline. Twenty years or so ago it was possible to photograph England's most charming and sequestered villages in such a way as to bring out their air of time-lessness and tradition; nowadays, every thatched or shingled roof, in no matter how isolated a hamlet, sprouts its television aerial, and all too much of the timeless charm is irretrievably sacrificed to this symbol of our century.

The same, on a vastly greater scale, has to be said of London. The capital may never have possessed, as Oxford did (and does), its 'dreaming spires': its extent was far too great for this to be taken in by the eye. But it had its indented skylines, each one differing from the next according to your viewpoint—whether it was the heights of Hampstead or the deck of a boat on the Thames. Now, though, and for ever more, the familiar and beloved skylines have been interrupted. Leaping skywards from among the turrets and cupolas, the steeples and domes, the crosses and sturdy towers and battlements, the historic figures perched on their lofty columns, these twentieth-century confirmations of man's questing spirit increasingly dominate the metropolitan scene.

When, just two centuries ago, the homely, country-loving poet, William Cowper, described the capital he knew as 'Opulent, enlarged and still increasing London', he wrote, in his eighteenth-century innocence, better than he knew. It was not a very poetic line; but its final words are borne out for us with every passing year. Indeed, thanks to the new skills as well as materials that are now available to our architects and builders, it seems that every passing month offers the wondering eye something spectacularly new. In a century's time, or even less, what, we may ask ourselves, perhaps with misgiving, will be the uppermost stratum of this historic palimpsest?

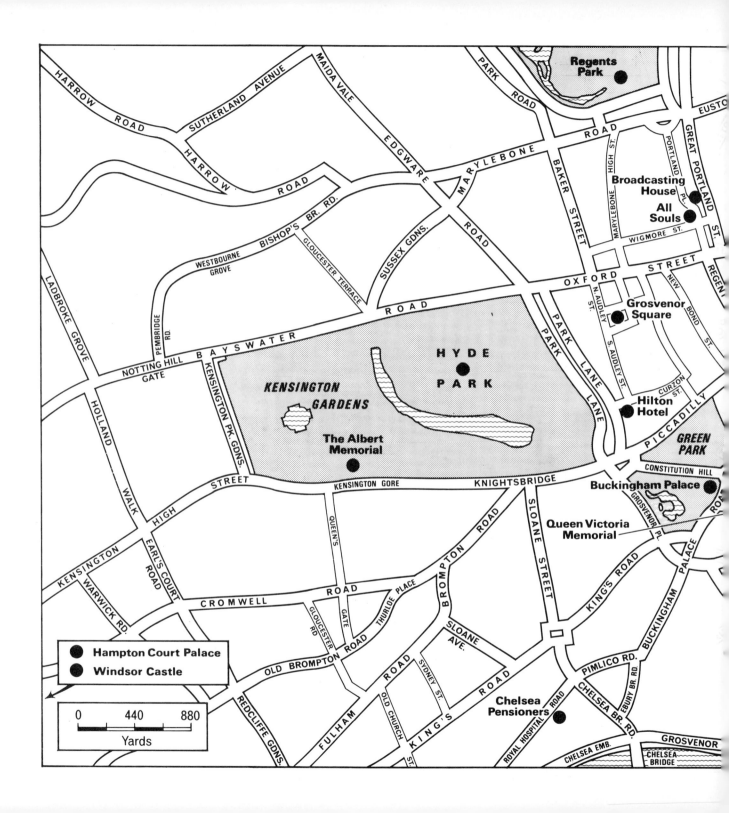

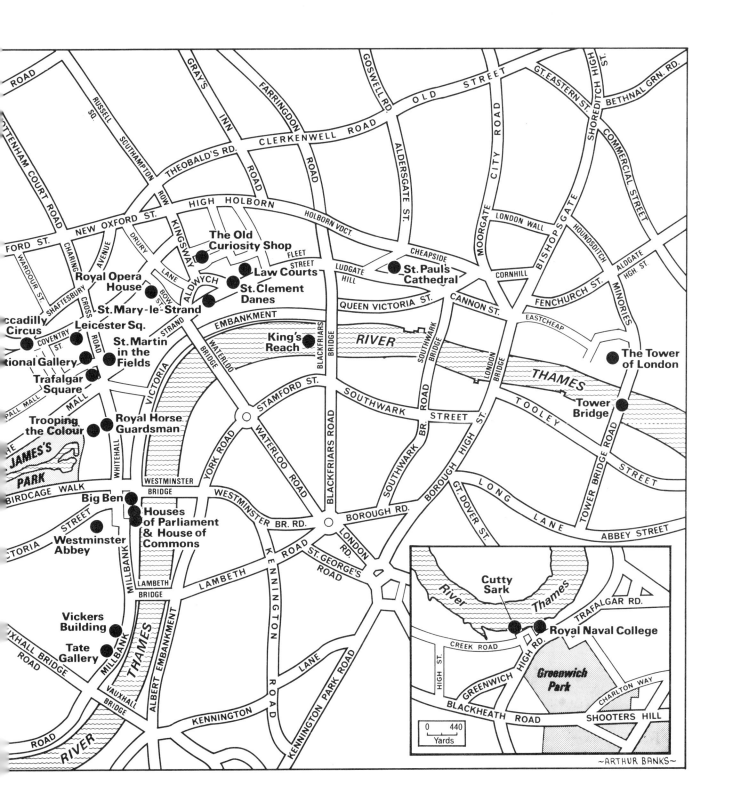

ROAD

RUSSELL SQ.

SOUTHAMPTON

THEOBALD'S RD.

GRAY'S INN ROAD

CLERKENWELL ROAD

FARRINGDON ROAD

GOSWELL RD.

OLD STREET

GT. EASTERN ST.

SHOREDITCH HIGH

BETHNAL GRN. RD.

COMMERCIAL STREET

CITY ROAD

MOORGATE

LONDON WALL

BISHOPSGATE

HOUNDSDITCH

TTENHAM COURT ROAD

HIGH HOLBORN

NEW OXFORD ST.

ROW

KINGSWAY

HOLBORN VDCT.

ALDERSGATE ST.

CORNHILL

FENCHURCH STREET

MINORIES

ALDGATE HIGH. ST.

FORD ST.

WARDOUR ST.

CHARING CROSS

AVENUE

DRURY LANE

BOW ST.

FLEET STREET

CHEAPSIDE

LUDGATE HILL

QUEEN VICTORIA ST.

CANNON ST.

EASTCHEAP

● **The Old Curiosity Shop**

Royal Opera House ●

● **Law Courts**

● **St. Clement Danes**

● **St. Paul's Cathedral**

SHAFTESBURY

● **St. Mary-le-Strand**

ALDWYCH

STRAND

● **The Tower of London**

ccadilly Circus ●

COVENTRY ST.

Leicester Sq. ●

● **St. Martin in the Fields**

EMBANKMENT

WATERLOO BRIDGE

BLACKFRIARS BRIDGE

● **King's Reach**

RIVER

SOUTHWARK BRIDGE

LONDON BRIDGE

THAMES

tional Gallery ●

● **Trafalgar Square**

VICTORIA

QUEEN VICTORIA ST.

● **Tower Bridge**

PALL MALL

MALL

● **Trooping the Colour**

● **Royal Horse Guardsman**

STAMFORD ST.

SOUTHWARK STREET

TOOLEY STREET

TOWER BRIDGE ROAD

JAMES'S PARK

WHITEHALL

YORK ROAD

WATERLOO ROAD

BLACKFRIARS ROAD

SOUTHWARK BR. ROAD

BOROUGH HIGH ST.

GT. DOVER ST.

LONG LANE

ABBEY STREET

BIRDCAGE WALK

● **Big Ben**

WESTMINSTER BRIDGE

BOROUGH RD.

STREET

● **Houses of Parliament & House of Commons**

WESTMINSTER BR. RD.

ICTORIA

● **Westminster Abbey**

MILLBANK

LAMBETH BRIDGE

LAMBETH ROAD

KENNINGTON ROAD

ST. GEORGE'S ROAD

LONDON RD.

● **Vickers Building**

● **Tate Gallery**

MILLBANK

THAMES

ALBERT EMBANKMENT

XHALL BRIDGE ROAD

VAUXHALL BRIDGE

KENNINGTON LANE

KENNINGTON PARK ROAD

ROAD

RIVER

KENNINGTON

River

Thames

Cutty Sark ●

● **Royal Naval College**

CREEK ROAD

HIGH ST.

GREENWICH

GREENWICH HIGH RD.

TRAFALGAR RD.

Greenwich Park

CHARLTON WAY

BLACKHEATH ROAD

SHOOTERS HILL

0   440
Yards

~ARTHUR BANKS~

THE PLATES

BIG BEN AND THE HOUSE OF COMMONS

Inevitably, the Houses of Parliament (even when dignified by being accorded their official title, Palace of Westminster) are dwarfed by the 320-foot clock tower, which carries one of the best-known clock faces in the world. The clock is almost universally known as Big Ben; in fact, it is the bell itself that is so named: a $13\frac{1}{2}$-ton bell named after the then First Commissioner of Works, Sir Benjamin Hall.

The four clock faces are set in 23-foot squares; the minute-hands are 14 feet long, and the figures are two feet high. The clock is an outstandingly good time-keeper, and an unusual feature is that it can be delicately adjusted by placing a coin in a shallow pan on the pendulum.

The Lower House adjoins the base of the Clock Tower. The thrusting statue facing it is that of Field-Marshal Jan Smuts, portrayed in this characteristic pose by Sir Jacob Epstein.

Même en portant le nom de Palais de Westminster, la House of Commons est anéantie devant la Clock Tower, plus connue sous le nom de Big Ben, nom de la cloche de $13\frac{1}{2}$ tonnes. Cette pendule est d'une exactitude remarquable.

Das Unterhaus wird von dem beinahe 110 m hohem Uhrturm, bekannt als Big Ben, überschattet. Aber nur die Glocke, nach Benjamin Hall benannt und $13\frac{1}{2}$ Tonnen wiegend, heisst eigentlich so.

THE HOUSES OF PARLIAMENT

Distance, it is said, lends enchantment to the view; certainly this neo-Gothic mass, designed by Sir Charles Barry in 1840 to replace an earlier building destroyed by fire after centuries of service, is seen at its best from upstream Lambeth Bridge.

It stretches for nearly 1,000 feet along the north bank of the river, from the 336-foot Victoria Tower to Westminster Bridge. When the House is in session, a Union Jack flies from the tower by day, and a light burns in the clock tower by night. M.P.s entertain their guests on the famous river-bank terrace.

They are occupying, whether in session or entertaining, hallowed ground. Here, nine centuries ago, stood Edward the Confessor's Palace of Westminster (hence the alternative title given to the Houses of Parliament). He bequeathed it 'in perpetuity' to his successors on the throne. Later monarchs, however, preferred different palace sites, and so abandoned this one.

Cette masse néo-gothique construite en 1840 par Sir Charles Barry le fut en remplacement d'un palais précédemment détruit par un incendie. 1000 pieds de long sur la rive nord de la Tamise—lorsque le parlement siège, le drapeau flotte, pendant la journée et la nuit, une lumière brille au sommet de Big Ben.

In neo-gotischem Stil gebaut wurde es 1840 von Sir Charles Barry entworfen, um das durch Feuer zerstörte alte Gebäude zu ersetzen. Wenn das Haus sitzt, fliegt am Tage die englische Fahne und bei Nacht brennt ein Licht in Uhrturm.

WESTMINSTER ABBEY

The building you see today stands on a site already hallowed by earlier ecclesiastical foundations long since mouldered away or destroyed. There was a Benedictine Abbey here more than 12 centuries ago. It was called 'Western Monastery', from which the accepted name derives, because it stood to the west of the City.

The first monarch to be buried here was that king-monk, Edward the Confessor. Since then, a long line of monarchs, statesmen, poets, dramatists and others have been brought to lie commemorated within these walls, beneath this splendid vaulted roof. And here, of course, all our monarchs are crowned.

Mainly, this is a supreme example of Early English architecture; this view, across Dean's Yard, is perhaps more memorable than the classic one of the West Front, for the eye is drawn rather to the graceful flying buttresses than to the massive twin towers that Hawksmoor added to the existing medieval concept in the eighteenth century.

Il y a 12 siècles, ce site fut celui d'une abbaye de bénédictins. Le premier monarque à y être enterré fut Edouard le Confesseur. Beaucoup d'autres personnages célèbres l'y ont suivi. C'est là aussi que les rois sont couronnés. C'est un superbe exemple d'architecture gothique britannique.

Diese Ansicht vom Deans Yard unterstreicht die frühenglische Architektur mehr als die Westansicht, da es die Aufmerksamkeit auf die Strebebögen und nicht auf die aus dem 18. Jahrhundert stammenden Westtürme lenkt.

THE NAVE, WESTMINSTER ABBEY

The graves and memorial slabs of monarchs and statesmen and philosophers and men of letters, explorers (such as Livingstone) and craftsmen (such as clock-maker Thomas Tompion), and distinguished men in half a hundred walks of life, all of them known by name and date, are to be found beneath the vaulted roof of this, the loftiest Gothic nave in England.

In the foreground of this picture, immediately inside the West Door, lies the grave of someone whose name and dates will never be known. It is that of an unidentified soldier of the First World War. This Unknown Warrior was brought here from Flanders and interred on Armistice Day, 1920. He represents 'the bravely dumb that did their deed and scorned to blot it with a name' in the 1914–1918 War.

Though interred amid hallowed stone, among the known great of his country, he sleeps in earth brought from the battlefield on which, anonymously, he breathed his last.

Au premier plan de cette photo se trouve le tombeau du Soldat Inconnu —dont l'enterrement eut lieu le jour de l'armistice en 1920. Sous les arches de cette superbe nef gothique, vous pourrez voir des tombes et plaques commémoratives de souverains, hommes d'état, philosophes, explorateurs, etc.

Unter dem gewölbten Dach dieses erhabenen Kirchenschiffes liegen die Gräber und Gedenksteine vieler berühmter Männer. Gleich beim Westeingang befindet sich das Grab des unbekannten Soldaten, der in 1920 hier beigesetzt wurde.

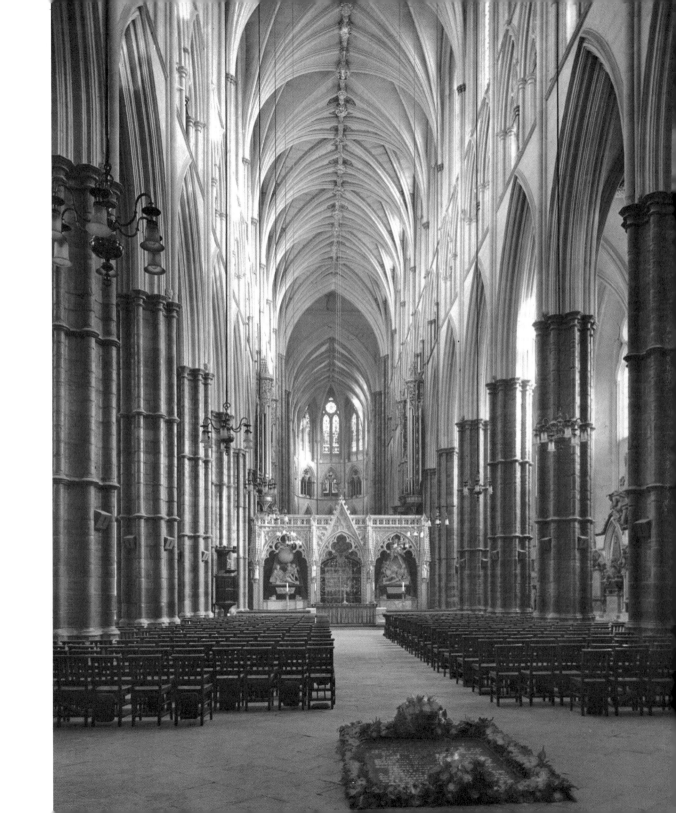

THAMES TIDEWAY

This dramatic view of the tideway downstream and eastwards from Westminster Bridge was taken from the top of the 336-foot Victoria Tower at the western end of the Palace of Westminster; it is virtually an aerial photograph.

Beyond Westminster Bridge is Charing Cross railway bridge, with the Hungerford footbridge running alongside; beyond that, gleaming white against the dark water and the massed trees on the Embankment, are the graceful arches of Sir Giles Scott's Waterloo Bridge, which replaced John Rennie's bridge in 1945.

The two bridges converge on the Royal Festival Hall and Queen Elizabeth Hall. The noon-day sun highlights the massed buildings on the North Bank: Shell-Mex House, Somerset House, churches galore and, just within view, the great dome and gilded cross of St Paul's.

Cette belle vue de la Tamise fut prise du sommet de Victoria Tower. Au delà de Westminster Bridge, il y a le pont de Charing Cross, pour trains et piétons, puis la masse blanche du Waterloo Bridge sur un fond d'eau sombre.

Aufgenommen von der Spitze des ungefähr 100 m hohen Viktoria Towers, gibt diese Fotografie einen wunderbaren Überblick über die verschiedenen Brücken und Gebäude am Themsekai.

ROYAL HORSE GUARDSMAN ON DUTY

Possibly the most footworn piece of pavement in all London is in Whitehall, immediately opposite the twin sentry-boxes at the Horse Guards; here, immobile, impassive, expressionless, are two mounted sentries, raised sword in hand, interminably gawped-at.

They are relieved (as shown in this picture) every hour. In this case a Royal Horse Guardsman (recognisable by his blue cloak and red plume) by a Life Guardsman (recognisable by his scarlet cloak and white plume).

What are they guarding? The buildings behind them form the grandiose Office of the Commander-in-Chief of the Home Forces. One suspects, however, that they are there because of our ingrained love of traditional ceremonial. Certainly the half-hour ceremony at mid-morning, when the Guard is relieved, is one that holds its rapt audience in thrall as much as that of Trooping the Colour on the Parade Ground to the rear of those massive buildings.

Le trottoir le plus usé de Londres est celui de Whitehall devant les postes de garde des Horse Guards. Les Royal Horse Guards en uniformes bleus et plumes rouges et les Life Guards en rouge et plumes blanches, veillent sur les bureaux du Commandeur en chef des forces armées. La relève de la garde est une cérémonie traditionnelle très populaire.

Diese Wachen vor dem Haus der Horse Guards werden täglich von 10 bis 16 Uhr aufgestellt und stündlich abgelöst. Besonders interessant ist die Zeremonie um 11 Uhr, die ungefähr $\frac{1}{2}$ Stunde dauert.

TROOPING THE COLOUR

This ceremony is one of the most magnificently staged of all displays of military pageantry in this country—perhaps anywhere in the world. It is held annually on the reigning monarch's 'official' birthday, which is the second Saturday in June.

Her Majesty Queen Elizabeth II is Colonel-in-Chief of the Life Guards, the Royal Horse Guards, the Grenadier, Coldstream, Scots, Irish and Welsh Guards. Wearing the uniform of one of these regiments, she rides, attended by a Sovereign's Mounted Escort, from Buckingham Palace to Horse Guards Parade. There she inspects the Guards, to the music of massed bands, and takes the salute.

Afterwards, she returns to the Palace at the head of the Guards deputed to mount the Palace Guard. Only one Colour is 'trooped' annually, that of each regiment in strict rotation. Originally it was called 'Lodging' the Colour: each regiment's own Colour being laid up, to music known as a 'Troop'.

Ce magnifique déploiement de faste militaire a lieu annuellement, le jour officiel de l'anniversaire du monarque—le deuxième samedi de juin. Sa Majesté la Reine Elizabeth II est vêtue, pour cette occasion, d'un des uniformes des régiments dont elle est Colonel en Chef.

Jedes Jahr zum offiziellen Geburtstag des regierenden Monarchen findet diese glänzende Zeremonie statt. Nur eine Fahne von den vielen verschiedenen Regimenten wird jedes Jahr abgenommen.

THE NATIONAL GALLERY and
ST MARTIN-IN-THE-FIELDS

The early nineteenth-century National Gallery, with its fine Corinthian columns (taken from a palace built for the Prince Regent), and the early eighteenth-century church of St Martin-in-the-Fields look askance at one another across the north-east corner of Trafalgar Square. Watkins's dome and unassuming lantern above are perhaps gently mocked by the impudent needle-spire which James Gibbs thought fit to mount 'unconformably', as the geologists say, upon his Corinthian portico.

Distributed among a score of well-lit rooms there is an outstandingly varied collection of paintings from British, Italian, Spanish, French, Dutch, Flemish and other famous schools. It is an international rather than, as named, a National Gallery.

In the church is the famous Crypt, once a burial-vault, and inter-mittently a place of refuge for the down-and-out. A macabre feature, often missed, is the parish 'whipping-post', once found in every country parish. But then, it *is* the church of St Martin 'in the fields', though these are now stone-overlaid.

La National Gallery construite au 19 e siècle avec ses fines colonnes corinthiennes et St Martin-in-the-Fields (18e siècle) se regardent en biais, à l'angle nord-est de Trafalgar Square. Au long des multiples salles, on peut admirer des chefs d'oeuvre 'internationaux' multiples.

Die im frühen 19. Jahrhundert erbaute Gallerie mit den schönen korinthischen Säulen und die aus dem 18. Jahrhundert stammende Kirche (Architekt Gibbs) stehen sich schräg in der Nord-Ostecke von Trafalgar Square gegenüber.

TRAFALGAR SQUARE BY NIGHT

It is ironic that Sir Robert Peel (founder of our police force) should have called the site where, in these restless days, so many police are involved in dealing with potentially riotous assemblies, 'the finest site in Europe'. Paris's Place de la Concorde may not agree, or Lisbon's Praça dos Restauradores; but it is undoubtedly a superb square, built where once the Royal Mews proliferated.

It is dominated by the 17-foot statue of Nelson on a 167-foot granite column, steadied, against the shock-waves of demonstrators, by Landseer's bronze lions, cast from the bronze of captured French guns.

The fairy-light-bedecked Christmas Tree, seen here from the National Gallery portico, is an annual gift from the Norwegian people; they try to make each year's gift a foot longer than its predecessor. How beautifully it is here contrasted with the black filigree-work of the traditional London plane tree.

Dénomée par Sir Robert Peel le plus beau site en Europe, ce dont on pourrait douter si l'on pense entre autres à la Place de la Concorde, cette place est néanmoins imposante, avec la statue de Nelson perchée sur la colonne de 167 pieds et flanquée des lions en bronze de Landseer, fondus dans le bronze des armes prises aux français. L'arbre de Noël est un don annuel du peuple norvégien.

Auf einer ungefähr 50 m hohen Granitsäule steht Nelson, zu seinen Füssen zwei Löwen aus Bronze von eroberten französischen Kanonen gegossen. Der Weihnachtsbaum ist ein Geschenk der Norweger.

48

BUCKINGHAM PALACE

There is justification for the familiar term, 'Buck House', for this London Palace stands on the site of Buckingham House, built in 1703 by the Duke of Buckingham and sold to George III in 1762. The first monarch, however, to take up residence here was Queen Victoria. Edward VII was born, and died, here.

The 'front' seen here, with the balcony on which Royalty occasionally appear before their loyal citizens, is not the true front; this is on the opposite side, overlooking the spacious grounds in which the Royal Garden Parties are held.

There has been much rebuilding of the great façade over the years; what confronts you today is largely due to Sir Aston Webb. In the North Wing (to the right of the picture) the Royal Family have their apartments. When, as here, the Royal Standard flies at the mast-head you will know that they are in residence.

Construit en 1703 par le Duc de Buckingham, vendu à George III en 1762, 'Buck House' ne fut pas réellement habité avant l'ère de la reine Victoria. La grande façade a été modernisée par Sir Aston Webb. La famille royale habite dans l'aile nord du palais et lorsque la reine est au palais, l'étendard est hissé.

In circa 1825 baute Nash Buckingham Haus (erbaut 1703) für George IV um, aber erst Königin Viktoria bezog diesen Palast, und die jetzige königliche Familie benutzt den Nordflügel als Residenz.

THE QUEEN VICTORIA MEMORIAL

This memorial was unveiled ten years after the queen's death in 1901. Her own statue is a seated figure on the far side, looking down The Mall; she has turned her back on Buckingham Palace, which she was the first monarch to reside in.

It is a highly symbolic creation (sometimes irreverently termed 'wedding-cake sculpture'). Allegorical representations of Truth and Justice, 'Motherhood and Peace, Art and Progress, Agriculture and Industry and Science, and Military and Naval (but not Air) Power surround her on all sides. The dominant feature is that of a gilded bronze figure of Winged Victory, flanked by Courage and Constancy.

Marching in through the main gateway is a detachment of the Palace Guards, some of those who go through the daily ceremonial of 'Changing the Guard at Buckingham Palace' before an audience that never ceases to delight in this spectacle which age cannot wither nor custom stale.

Ce monument fut dévoilé 10 ans après la mort de la Reine en 1901. De là, elle contemple le Mall et tourne le dos à Buckingham, qu'elle fut la première à habiter. Création très symbolique, avec de nombreuses allégories, dont une figure en bronze doré de la Victoire Ailée, en compagnie du Courage et de la Constance.

Zehn Jahre nach dem Tode (1901) der Königin wurde dieses Ehrenmal enthüllt. Viktoria, umgeben von allegorischen Figuren, hat Buckingham Palace den Rücken zugekehrt und sieht den Pall Mall hinunter.

THE THAMES BY NIGHT

Strictly functional, ever busy, even slightly menacing with its impression of sheer bulk and seaward-flowing purposefulness, London's River (in remote geological times a mere tributary of the Rhine) assumes a wholly different mantle when darkness has fallen and the lights prick out to match the stars overhead: magic is not too fanciful a word for it.

Here, looking upstream from a point above Waterloo Bridge, even the utilitarian (and admittedly unlovely) Charing Cross Railway Bridge acquires a certain massive charm. Beyond are the graceful spans of Westminster Bridge, the last of them thrusting boldly to the very threshold of the Palace of Westminster.

Beyond the Houses of Parliament there soars into the night-hazy sky the monolithic Millbank Tower. It is a night skyline that might have inspired Wordsworth once again.

Rivière purement fonctionnelle et occupée, le jour, la Tamise revêt un autre aspect, le soir. Même le pont purement utilitaire de Charing Cross acquiert alors un certain charme. Derrière, on aperçoit le Palais de Westminster, puis plus loin, Millbank Tower.

Wenn es dunkel wird, verändert sich die sonst bei Tage so geschäftige und nüchterne Themse, und die Lichter verzaubern sogar unschöne Ansichten, wie die Charing Cross Eisenbahnbrücke.

PICCADILLY CIRCUS

Somewhat grandiloquently called 'the hub of the Empire'—or even 'of the Universe'—this awkwardly shaped meeting-point of half-a-dozen notable streets, including curved Regent Street to the north-west and the mile-long arrow-length of Piccadilly to the south-west, has become the lodestone that draws visitors from the six continents.

It is also the supreme example of brash contemporary advertising, a tacit-visual declaration of Mammon's stranglehold on Man.

At its heart, utterly unrelated to its surroundings save in so far as it commemorates the philanthropic Earl of Shaftesbury, whose name is borne by the avenue curving away north-eastwards, is the exquisite little winged statue of the Angel of Christian Charity, universally (but erroneously) known as 'Eros'. On occasions when rioting (good-humoured or otherwise) is anticipated, Authority encloses him in armour. Perhaps another Authority will eventually implement a tentative scheme for saving Piccadilly Circus from destroying itself.

Carrefour d'une demi-douzaine de rues célèbres, cette place est devenue le point de rendez-vous des visiteurs des six continents. Au centre de cette place, qui est l'exemple même de la publicité moderne vulgaire, se tient l'Ange de la Charité Chrétienne (faussement connu sous le nom d'Eros).

Dieser Platz, wo sechs wohlbekannte Strassen sich treffen, ist zum Magneten für Besucher aus aller Welt geworden. In der Mitte befindet sich eine Statue volkstümlich als 'Eros' bekannt.

LEICESTER SQUARE

It takes a discerning eye (and a good lens) to locate this most pleasant oasis of dappled greenery in the still centre of this pulsing and tumultuous Square, set about with monolithic edifices. First World War soldiers in their marching-song bade 'goodbye' to Piccadilly, but 'farewell' to Leicester Square.

There is another, and subtler, link. The Square takes its name from the former Town House of the Earls of Leicester; the country house is in the Kentish village of Penshurst, which possesses a minuscule 'Leicester Square', pocket-handkerchief-size, to this day.

In Leicester Fields, spacious garden of the Town House, duels were fought, where now a statue to Shakespeare broods over the tulip beds beneath plane trees planted almost a century ago when the garden was magnanimously 'presented to the people of London' by the dubious 'Baron Grant' (or Gottheimer) shortly before his ignominious exposure for fraud.

Un petit oasis de verdure et de fraîcheur au milieu de ce quartier si tumultueux. Cette place tient son nom du Duc de Leicester, qui avait une maison à Penhurst, dans le jardin de laquelle il y a, encore de nos jours, un Leicester Square miniature.

Dieser Platz bezieht seinen Namen von dem ehemaligen Stadthaus des Grafen von Leicester; und in Leicester Fields wurden Duelle ausgetragen. Jetzt steht dort zwischen Platanen eine Statue von Shakespeare.

ROYAL OPERA HOUSE, COVENT GARDEN

Familiarly known as 'Covent Garden', it is the third to have been built on this site in what was originally the 'Convent Garden of St Peter's'—the famous flower, fruit and vegetable market whose days on this historic site are now, alas, numbered. It stands directly opposite Bow Street Police Court, premier of London's 14 Metropolitan Courts.

Traditionally the home of Grand Opera, it is here that the major opera and ballet productions are staged. Its 2,300 seats are eagerly competed for by opera-lovers and balletomanes, who willingly pick their way through the somewhat squalid approaches, in which crushed cabbage-stalks beneath the feet are matched by the composite odours of the market's produce decaying after a long day's trading and transport by the vociferous porters.

What a contrast: especially when, as here, Her Majesty is present in the Royal Box, flanked by her Yeoman Warder in his Tudor garb!

Connu sous le nom de Covent Garden, c'est le troisième opéra à être construit sur cet emplacement au coeur de ce marché historique. Les amateurs d'opéra et de ballet se pressent toujours d'occuper les 2.300 places et n'hésitent pas à traverser ce quartier parfois sale et malodorant. Quel contraste—surtout lorsque la reine occupe la loge royale, et que les gardes sont en somptueux uniformes de style Tudor.

Auch als Covent Garden bekannt, ist dieses Opernhaus das dritte, welches hier inmitten dem Gemüsegrossmarkt erbaut wurde. Direkt gegenüber befindet sich das berühmteste Londoner Polizeigericht—Bow Street Court.

ST MARY-le-STRAND and ST CLEMENT DANES

Both these well-loved churches stand on 'islands' in the Strand, with waves of traffic swirling continuously past them to starboard and port.

The more westerly is St Mary-le-Strand, built by the architect of St Martin-in-the-Fields to Queen Anne's order for 'Fifty New Churches'. This little beauty has been described as 'a casket one can handle with one's hands'; for all its Ionic portico, its balustrade and ornate stepped steeple, it possesses a charmingly Lilliputian quality.

Farther east, behind its shoulder, is the church of St Clement (the suffix 'Danes' cannot be substantiated). Wren built it, but James Gibbs added the elegant 115-foot tower. This contains the bells from which derives the nursery-rhyme, 'Oranges and lemons, Say the bells of St Clements'. Reconstructed after heavy bomb damage, it has appropriately been adopted by the R.A.F. as their own special London church.

Ces deux églises sont situées dans des îlots au coeur de Strand. A l'ouest, St Mary le Strand construite sur les ordres de Queen Anne, par l'architecte de St Martin-in-the-Fields. A l'est, St Clement. Construite par Wren, mais complétée par James Gibbs qui y ajouta la tour de 115 pieds.

Diese beiden Kirchen stehen auf 'Inseln' im Strand, der Verkehr flutet unablässig vorbei. St. Mary-le-Strand wurde in 1774 von Gibbs erbaut; und Wren entwarf und baute St. Clement Danes in 1680–82.

THE LAW COURTS

Officially styled the Royal Courts of Justice, this huge neo-Gothic building, not yet a century old, overlooks the junction of Fleet Street and The Strand, at Temple Bar.

Here are held the Courts of Probate, Divorce and Admiralty (strange bedfellows, surely?), of Chancery, Queen's Bench, and Appeal. The high drama of murder and other major crimes must be sought at the Old Bailey, to the east, off Newgate Street.

It is at the Royal Courts of Justice that, annually in November, the newly elected Lord Mayor of London must present himself to the Lord Chief Justice, deputising for the monarch, to swear that he will dutifully fulfil all those responsibilities that have become his by virtue of his high office. The oath sworn, he invites the Lord Chief Justice to be his dinner guest at Guildhall.

The shadowed figure in the foreground, contemplating the Law Courts and Fleet Street, is Dr Samuel Johnson, Londoner.

Répondant au titre officiel de 'Royal Courts of Justice', cet impressionnant édifice néo-gothique est situé à la jonction de Fleet Street et de Strand. C'est là qu'au mois de novembre, le nouveau Maire de Londres reçoit son investiture des mains du Lord Chief Justice.

Dieses grosse, neo-gotische Gerichtsgebäude, noch nicht ganz 100 Jahre alt, liegt an der Strassenmündung von Fleet Street und dem Strand in Temple Bar.

THE THAMES: KING'S REACH

Immediately upstream of London Bridge is the Pool of London; upstream of this is King's Reach, commemorating George V. Looking downstream from Westminster, you see a line of ships permanently moored against the Embankment. The first of these is Captain Scott's *Discovery*, the fine three-master in which he embarked in 1912 on his ill-fated South Pole expedition.

Astern of her lies the *Wellington*, the Livery Hall of the Master Mariners' Company. Astern of her lie two training ships, one of which, H.M.S. *President*, flies the admiral's flag when some admiral has been temporarily seconded to the Admiralty in near-by Whitehall.

The ships' masts are seen in pale silhouette against the massed trees of the beautiful Temple Gardens that separate Westminster from the City proper. Dominating an irregular skyline of ancient and modern is the great dome of St Paul's, whose gilded cross rises 365 feet from the ground.

En amont de London Bridge, il y a the Pool of London et puis, plus loin le King's Reach. Sur les quais en aval de Westminster, on peut reconnaître les bateaux suivants 'Discovery' du Captain Scott, puis le 'Wellington', puis deux navires d'apprentissage dont H.M.S. 'President'.

Die Themse zwischen Westminster und London wurde zur Erinnerung an George V in 1935 King's Reach benannt. Stromabwärts von Westminster liegen die Schiffe 'Discovery' und 'Wellington' und das Ubungsschiff H.M.S. 'President'.

ST PAUL'S CATHEDRAL

It is fitting that Sir Christopher Wren should have been the first man to be buried here, at the age of 91, for this is his greatest achievement. His tombstone bears a Latin inscription: 'If you seek my memorial, look about you'.

The building of this 'national cathedral of England' occupied him for 35 years. It stands on a site that knew several earlier churches, Saxon and Norman, the last of which was destroyed in the Great Fire of London, in 1666, and it miraculously survived the holocaust of 29 December 1940.

The right-hand tower contains the famous 17-ton bell, 'Great Paul'. Between the two west towers rises the famous dome containing the 'Whispering Gallery' and surmounted by the Golden Gallery, the Lantern, and the Ball and gilded Cross. By tradition, Westminster may be 'royalty's church'; but St Paul's belongs by right to the City of London and its faithful citizenry.

Sir Christopher Wren, dont ce fut la plus somptueuse création, fut le premier homme à y être enterré. Il lui fallut 35 ans pour construire 'la cathédrale nationale d'Angleterre'. La Tour de droite contient la fameuse cloche de 17 tonnes 'Great Paul'. Entre les deux tours, il y a le fameux dôme et la non moins fameuse galerie des murmures.

Die jetzige Kathedrale, entworfen von Wren und 35 Jahre von ihm überwacht, steht auf der selben Stelle wie frühere Kirchen, die letzte wurde beim grossen Feuer (1666) zerstört.

THE TOWER OF LONDON and TOWER BRIDGE

This 'Saga in Stone' is perhaps best seen from the South Bank, when the spectacular Tower Bridge (built eight centuries later) immediately opposite is less conspicuous. Best of all, of course, when floodlit.

William the Conqueror built this palimpsest of history on the seaward side of the existing city, as a token of his might and a warning to potential river-borne invaders. It has served as citadel and arsenal, royal palace and state prison, armoury, treasury and mint, for nine centuries. The ghosts of kings and queens and statesmen and generals and admirals and archbishops and traitors haunt the towers and dungeons and passages of this moated assemblage of virtually impregnable buildings.

To the left of the picture is part of the White Tower, the original Keep and oldest portion of the whole complex, rising 90 feet and with walls 15 feet thick; but Nature supplies her foil to the battlements.

Guillaume le Conquérant la construisit comme le symbole de sa puissance et comme un rappel aux envahisseurs éventuels. Elle servit successivement depuis neuf siècles de citadelle et d'arsenal, de palais et de prison, d'armurerie et de trésor. De multiples fantômes très nobles hantent ses tours et donjons.

'Geschichte in Stein', so kann man diese Festung, von Wilhelm dem Eroberer erbaut, nennen. Links sehen Sie einen Teil des White Towers, das ursprüngliche Burgverlies und ältester Teil des Gebäudekomplexes.

ROYAL NAVAL COLLEGE, GREENWICH

A royal palace originally graced this river-bank site. Here Henry VIII was born, married two of his wives, and signed Anne Boleyn's death-warrant. Here, too, were born his daughters, Elizabeth and Mary.

Later it became a home for disabled and pensioned sailors, the maritime counterpart of the Chelsea Royal Hospital; known as Greenwich Hospital, it fulfilled this function until 1869, when it became a college for the advanced education of naval officers.

What confronts you today is largely the work of Wren, though parts of the huge complex are the work of Vanbrugh and Hawksmoor. Immediately behind is a low-pitched white building, the Queen's House, designed by Inigo Jones for James I's Queen, Anne of Denmark. Two open colonnades link this with the main building and will lead you to one of London's newest major museums, the National Maritime Museum.

C'est là qu'Henry VIII naquit, épousa deux de ses femmes et signa l'arrêt de mort d'Anne Boleyn. C'est là aussi que naquirent deux de ses filles Elizabeth et Mary. Cette demeure devint par la suite un hôpital pour marins jusqu'en 1869, date à laquelle il fut transformé en collège pour les officiers de marine.

Dieses Gebäude, hauptsächlich von Wren entworfen, hat eine bewegte Geschichte, denn es diente als ein Palast (Henry VIII), dann als Hospital für pensionierte Seeleute (Greenwich Hospital bis 1869), und letztlich als Seekadettenschule.

THE CUTTY SARK

She was one of the most famous of all the great tea-clippers; her heyday, like that of the great grain-carrying clippers on the Australia run, was little more than a century ago.

Until 1954 she was somewhat ignominiously berthed at Greenhithe; but in that year she was ceremonially brought upriver to a new berth right opposite the former Royal Palace (birthplace of Henry VIII) at Greenwich, now the National Maritime Museum.

Though essentially an educational centre for the Merchant Navy, she is herself a museum—of ships' figureheads and other objects with a powerful nautical association. Her voluminous sails have gone, but her great masts and yardarms and complex rigging are still as they were when she was breasting the oceans of the world. And beneath her keel runs Meridian 0 of Longitude, fundamental navigation-point for the pilots of the world's shipping.

Un des plus célèbres clippers, il fut ancré à Greenhithe jusqu'en 1954, puis amené à Greenwich, en face de l'ancien palais royal—aujourd'hui Musée National de la Marine. Centre éducatif de la Marine Marchande, le Cutty Sark est aussi un véritable musée de tout ce qui peut symboliser la marine.

Einst der berühmteste Tee-Klipper, liegt die Cutty Sark jetzt in Greenwich gegenüber dem Seefahrtsmuseum. Unter dem Kiel verläuft der O Längengrad.

THE OLD CURIOSITY SHOP

This unexpected survival of an early seventeenth-century (or, as it claims, late sixteenth-century) building lurks in Portsmouth Street, between Portugal Street and Lincoln's Inn Fields. Traditionally, it is the original of Dicken's *Old Curiosity Shop* (1841), where Little Nell lived with her grandfather until the evil Mr Quilp forced them to flee.

In fact, the true original was almost certainly in Charing Cross Road, near the site of the statue of Sir Henry Irving, Actor. It is therefore more interesting as a rare survival of a genuine village structure than as a dubious original immortalised by a novelist.

A 'village' structure? The clue lies in the reference to Lincoln's Inn *Fields* (and in St Martin-in-the-*Fields*, not so far away). High Holborn has its (reconstructed) medieval timber building, Staple Inn; but this is on a more ambitious scale (though of almost the same date) than this little shop.

Datant du 17ème siècle, ce serait soi-distant la véritable Old Curiosity Shop de Charles Dickens où Little Nell vécut avec son grand-père. Ceci est peu probable, car l'original était situé près de Charing Cross. C'est plutôt ce qu'il nous reste d'un vrai village ancien.

Dieses alte Gebäude aus dem frühen 17. Jahrundert befindet sich in Portsmouth Street, und es wird davon gesagt, dass es das Original für Dickens 'Old Curiosity Shop' war.

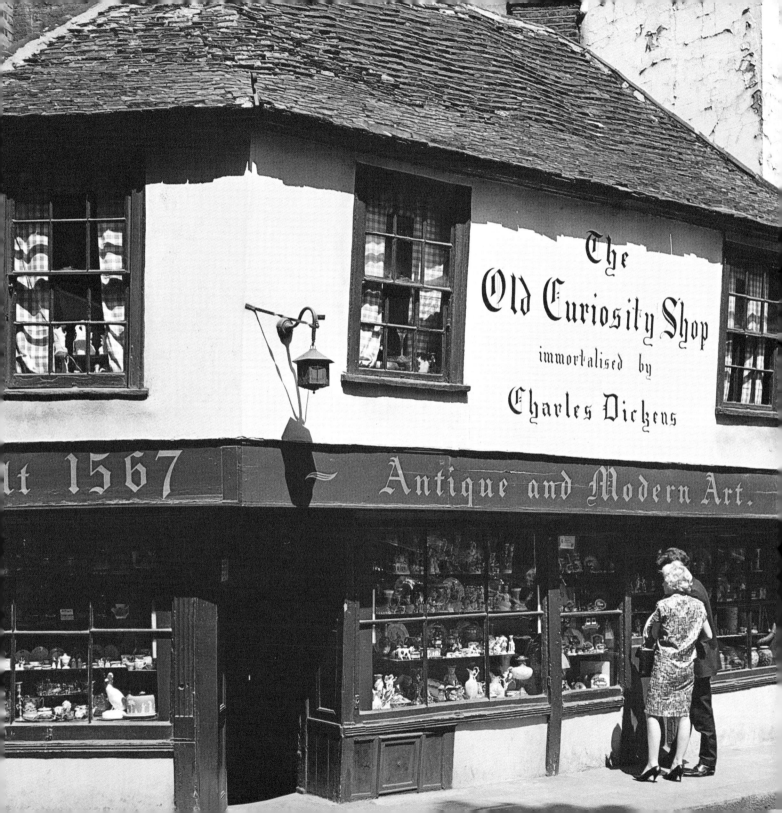

BROADCASTING HOUSE and ALL SOULS' CHURCH

In 1931, Val Myer's and Watson Hart's new Broadcasting House, at the upper extremity of Regent Street, was regarded by most conventional people as ultra-modern. The blunt 'bows' of this enormous stone vessel, apparently about to be launched southwards from Portland Place, carry a sculptured group by Eric Gill.

The monolithic figure of the humourless Prospero can be accepted; but can Ariel, his 'tricksy spirit', really be captured in stone? Anyway, after four decades this once-modern building already seems antique in contrast with the Millbank Tower and other skyward-rearing edifices.

Save possibly to those who earn their livelihood within its bulk it will never be as dear to Londoners as Nash's exquisitely designed All Souls' Church close by. With its pillared portico, its balustrade, its pillared drum and soaring fluted needle-like spire, it forms a perfect contrast to its elephantine neighbour. Ariel, surely, belongs here?

En 1931, Broadcasting House, construite par Val Myer et Watson Hart, était considéré comme un immeuble ultra-moderne. Aujourd'hui, comparé aux gratte-ciel comme Millbank Tower, Broadcasting House a bien vieilli. Tout à côté, construite par Nash, se situe la ravissante église, All Souls' Church, dont il faut noter le portique à piliers, la balustrade et le clocher en pointe.

Dieses einst ultra-moderne Gebäude (Architekten Val Myer und Watson Hart) liegt am obersten Ende von Regent Street. Ganz in der Nähe befindet sich die exquisite, von Nash entworfene 'All Souls'.

REGENT'S PARK

Like Hyde Park, filched from the Benedictine Monks of Westminster by Henry VIII, this was originally part of his Royal Hunting Park. Extending to nearly 500 acres, it was later disciplined by Nash as a garden for a country mansion which the Prince Regent planned to build here. Regent Street was intended by Nash as a through-way between his Carlton House and this house-and-garden-to-be.

The public have had access to it for well over a century. The Zoo fills one corner; near the centre is Queen Mary's Garden, enclosing the Open Air Theatre; on the south-west curve there is a 20-acre boating lake of unusual shape, surrounded by gravel walks, variegated trees and flower beds.

Look inward from the periphery, and you would believe yourself on a spacious village green; look outwards, and some of the most distinguished terrace-houses in all London form the skyline. *Rus*, you might truly say, *in urbe*.

Henry VIII, après l'avoir pris aux Moines Bénédictins, en fit son parc de chasse. Plus tard, Nash en fit le jardin de la maison de campagne que le Prince Regent avait envisagé de faire construire. Depuis un siècle, il est ouvert au public. Il comporte, entre autres, un zoo et le jardin de la Reine Mary, avec son théâtre en plein air.

Der von Nash angelegte Park war ursprünglich Teil des Jagdreviers Henry VIII und ist beinahe 500 Morgen gross. Besondere Merkmale sind ein grossangelegter Zoo und Queen Mary's Garten mit Freilichtbühne.

GROSVENOR SQUARE

There is an air not only of spaciousness but of respectability, of dignity, about this great square that is not to be found in certain other, and more popular squares. The whole of its west side is flanked by the enormous United States Embassy. But its gigantic American Eagle is entirely hidden by a tracery of twigs on a still leafless tree.

The statue of F. D. Roosevelt on the north side is silhouetted against the mellow brickwork of other important buildings, and he looks across to the Embassy that he never knew, which overlooks six acres of good turf criss-crossed with paths and dappled with flower beds, formerly the site of an extensive earthwork thrown up by Londoners in haste to forestall Charles II's march on London.

The name comes from one of England's oldest families, dating back to Norman times, but ennobled a century ago to become Earls of Westminster and landowners on the heroic scale.

Cette superbe et imposante place doit son nom à l'une des plus anciennes familles britanniques: the Earls of Westminster. Sur le côté ouest du square, l'aigle américain veille sur l'énorme ambassade des Etats-Unis. Au nord, la statue de F. D. Roosevelt domine le square de pelouses et plate-bandes fleuries.

Dieser Platz ist nach einer der ältesten englischen Familien benannt; und die ganze Westseite dieses Platzes wird von der amerikanischen Botschaft eingenommen. Auf der Nordseite befindet sich die Statue von F. D. Roosevelt.

THE TATE GALLERY and THE VICKERS BUILDING

Behold as effective a contrast in architectural styles in juxtaposition as could be imagined! They stand on Millbank, on the north bank of the river between Vauxhall Bridge and Lambeth Bridge.

The Tate Gallery, designed in 'free classical style', was opened in 1897. It stands on the site of the notorious Millbank Penitentiary and in its score and more galleries the emphasis is on the British schools of painting of the last 400 years, though masterpieces from other countries are also to be found in profusion.

Looming behind and above it is Britain's handsomest skyscraper, completed in 1962. Its official name is Millbank Tower, but it is generally known otherwise because of the distinguished occupiers of much of its vast space. At 387 feet it is the highest skyscraper in the country, though it is eclipsed easily by the 580-foot Post Office Tower. But it is, surely, infinitely more elegant, even if less slender.

La Tate Gallery, conçue dans un style classique libre, fut inaugurée en 1897. Dans ses multiples galeries, l'accent est mis sur les écoles britanniques de peinture des 4 derniers siècles. En arrière, le plus beau gratte-ciel britannique construit en 1962. Connu sous le nom de Millbank Tower, ses 387 pieds ne sont éclipsés que par les 580 pieds de la Post Office Tower.

Beide Gebäude sind in Millbank zu finden; die Tate Gallerie, im Jahre 1897 eröffnet, beherbergt hauptsächlich britische Künstler. Millbank Tower ist mit etwa 100 m leicht das höchste Gebäude in England.

CHELSEA PENSIONERS

This 'conversation piece' is composed of three of the 480-odd inmates of Chelsea's Royal Hospital, founded at the instigation of Charles II as a retreat for aged and disabled soldiers.

Wearing the traditional summer uniform, dating from Marlborough's campaigns, a Warrant Officer (with Royal Crown badge on his sleeve) stands between a tall Sergeant and a be-medalled In-patient. In the winter they wear dark blue. Their tricorns are worn on occasions such as Oak Apple Day (29 May), when they celebrate the birthday of their Royal Founder, whose statue, by Grinling Gibbons, stands in the Centre Court.

Sir Christopher Wren designed the Hospital, and its foundation-stone was laid by the king himself, in 1682. The severely elegant façade consists of two wings built in dark but mellow brick enclosing a somewhat stark portico in grey-white stone faced with Doric pillars, the whole somewhat relieved by the eight well-proportioned windows.

Cette conversation réunit trois des 480 pensionnaires du Chelsea Royal Hospital, créé à la demande de Charles II pour les soldats retraités. Sir Christopher Wren en fut l'architecte et le roi même en posa la première pierre en 1682.

Diese drei uniformierten Pensionäre gehören dem königlichen Chelsea Krankenhaus an, ein Altersheim für dienstunfähige oder kriegsversehrte Soldaten. Im Jahre 1682 legte Charles II den Grundstein für das von Wren entworfene Krankenhaus.

THE ALBERT MEMORIAL

You may not approve the comment, made when this memorial to Queen Victoria's Consort, Prince Albert of Saxe-Coburg-Gotha, was erected in 1876, that it is 'beyond question the finest monumental structure in Europe'; the speaker had perhaps not been, for instance, to Rome.

The sheer mass of its assembled detail, however, must evoke reluctant admiration. Albert is engrossed in the Catalogue of the Great Exhibition of 1851 (for which he was largely responsible). He is surrounded by allegorical figures, blood-relations of those on the Queen's own Memorial outside Buckingham Palace.

Whiter-than-white Italian marble contrasts sunnily with dark bronze; and there are less usual materials here: 'agate, onyx, jasper, cornelian, crystal and other richly coloured substances', you will find. The Victorians did nothing by halves, and their sorrowing monarch's requests were words-of-command. Sir George Gilbert Scott carried them out to the letter, interpreting them on his own initiative.

Sans être, comme quelqu'un l'avait dit, lors de sa construction en 1876, le plus beau monument d'Europe, cette énorme masse est assez admirable. Le marbre blanc de blanc italien crée un contraste frappant avec le bronze sombre et les autres multiples matériaux . . . agate, onyx, etc.

Dieses in 1876 von Scott ausgeführte Ehrenmal aus schneeweissem italienischen Marmor ist sehr reich in Einzelheiten. Prinz Albert hat sich in einen Katalog von der 'Grossen Ausstellung in 1851' vertieft und ist von allegorischen Figuren umgeben.

HYDE PARK and the HILTON HOTEL

'Tip-toe among the tulips', you might be tempted to quote, glancing at this picture. The tulip bed is, of course, just one of the many features that make this 360-acre stretch of parkland, right in the heart of London, so attractive throughout spring and summer.

And on tip-toe in the background are the upper ten storeys of the Hilton Hotel, more than 300 feet high and containing some 500 bedrooms in addition to a multiplicity of restaurants, bars and other public rooms. They are certainly all 'rooms with a view'!

It is a curious thought that this best-loved of all London's parks originally belonged to the Benedictine Monks of the 'Western Monastery'; at the Dissolution, that unscrupulous opportunist Henry VIII seized it and turned it into a Royal Hunting Park. The last deer, descendants of those that had been royally hunted, disappeared little more than a century ago.

Ce magnifique parterre de tulipes est un des multiples attraits de ce superbe parc au coeur de Londres. En fond de décor, l'hôtel Hilton avec ses quelque 500 chambres avec une vue imprenable. Ce parc appartenait aux Moines Bénédictins jusqu'à ce qu'Henry VIII en fasse son parc ce chasse privé.

So wie Regent's Park wurde auch dieser beliebte Park den Benediktiner Mönchen enteignet und bekam Jagdrevier Henry VIII. Im Hintergrund das beinahe 100 m hohe Gebäude des Londoner Hiltons.

HAMPTON COURT PALACE

Overweening and ill-fated Cardinal Wolsey planned for himself what was to be the most ambitious private residence in England. He over-reached himself, tried to regain Henry VIII's favour by offering his monarch this gift-under-duress; he lost his palace but failed to mend his fortunes.

Henry VIII added the Great Hall and Chapel, and Hampton was a favourite Royal Residence for two centuries. Edward VI was born there; William III died as a result of a fall in its parkland.

The magnificent mellow brick-and-stone façade seen here, over-looking the Thames 13 miles upstream from London, is largely the work of Wren, whose signature in London is ubiquitous. No longer a palace, but a former Royal Residence now open to all, it ranks as one of the finest showpieces within hail of the metropolis: yet another of the innumerable examples of history writ in brick and stone, haunted by those who knew it in its heyday.

Ce fut la résidence privée de l'ambitieux et malchanceux Cardinal Wolsey. Il voulut en faire don à Henry VIII pour rentrer en faveur. Il y perdit sa demeure et ne fut pas pardonné. Henry VIII y ajouta le 'Great Hall' et la Chapelle et ce fut la demeure royale préférée pendant deux siècles. La façade fut l'oeuvre de Wren.

Dieser grossartig angelegte Palast, 13 Meilen stromaufwärts von London, war von Kardinal Wolsey als seine Residenz geplant, er schenkte ihn dann aber Henry VIII in der Hoffnung, seine Gunst damit wiederzuerlangen.

WINDSOR CASTLE

Not strictly in London, of course, for it is situated 20-odd miles up-stream from the metropolis. But it is the monarch's nearest country residence and, incidentally, the oldest of them all. Also, not only is it England's premier castle but it is the largest inhabited castle in the world.

This view of it across the Thames shows the Royal Standard flying: this denotes that the monarch is in residence. It flies from a turret on the magnificent Keep, known as the Round Tower, built by Henry II to replace the original timber structure built by William the Conqueror.

Successive kings built and rebuilt, elaborated and added, extended the curtain-walls, threw up the immense polygonal towers, deepened the dungeons. Few castles, at least of this stature, are more finely sited than this complex of massive buildings crowning the precipice-like bluff whose foot is washed by London's river.

A environ 30 km de Londres, c'est la plus ancienne des résidences royales. De nombreux rois l'ont transformé, y ont ajouté des tours, creusé des donjons. Peu de châteaux sont si bien situés, dominant la rivière et permettant d'obtenir une vue comme celle-ci.

Dieses älteste aller Schlösser ist die nahegelegenste ländliche Residenz, und auf dieser Fotografie kann man die Standarte vom runden Turm fliegen sehen, was heisst, dass die königliche Familie dort augenblicklich residiert.